Account of the Ionic Trophy Monument Excavated at Xanthus

ACCOUNT

OF THE

IONIC TROPHY MONUMENT

EXCAVATED AT

XANTHUS.

BY

SIR CHARLES FELLOWS.

.

LONDON:

JOHN MURRAY, ALBEMARLE STREET.

MDCCCXLVIII.

IONIC TROPHY MONUMENT

AT XANTHUS.

We learn from Herodotus* that the people called by the Greeks Lycians, were by the early inhabitants of the country known by the name of Termelæ, and that even in the time of that historian, 450 B.C., the people were called Termilians by their neighbours. Other ancient authors† call them Termilæ and Tramilæ. The name of Lycia was applied by the Greeks to the country, and that of Xanthus designated the chief city; but both names seem to have been unknown to the people of the country. In the numerous inscriptions found on the monuments, the chief city is called Arina‡, and the country Tramelæ§. To this earliest people are to be attributed the rock-tombs, which are of the same succession of dates as the detached architectural monu-

---

* Lib. i. cap. 173; lib. vii. cap. 92.
† Stephanus Byzantinus. ‡ Ibid.
§ This name is seen in almost every inscription in the early language.

B

ments, the sculpture and the language,—all characterized as peculiar to this country; the coins, sculptured
legends and mythology all belong to the same people.
These are the earliest works seen in the country*.

The ancient city of Arina stood principally upon a
bold rock rising abruptly from the river Xanthus. It is
upon this Acropolis that we find exclusively the ruins of
the monuments of the early inhabitants. The walls, the
towers, the peculiar stele†, the gothic-shaped tombs, and
tombs sculptured to imitate wood-work, are all still to
be seen on this site. It is surprising, and highly interesting, that we should have been made so well acquainted with the appearance, character and architecture
of the cities of this early people, by the numerous views
of the ancient cities of Pinara, Tlos, and even of Arina
or Xanthus itself, sculptured in bas-relief; from the
sculpture we also learn the costume,—the loose robe,
the beard, the short sword, the bow-case, the construction of their chariots and peculiar trappings of their
horses; we have also presented to us their poetic legends, recorded in the poems of Homer, and the often-
repeated mythological allusions in the funereal ceremo

* The rocks of Lycia are scaglia or Apennine limestone, extremely
hard and flinty, and difficult to cut; but when sculptured they retain a
sharp edge for an interminable period. Many of the earliest sculptures
retain their painted surface to the present day. It is therefore impossible to conceive the work of a former people passing entirely away,
when those of twenty-five centuries ago appear as of yesterday.

† ‘Lycia,’ p. 104.

nies. A knowledge of the peculiarities of this people, obtained from a close examination of their works, will throw much light upon the subject of these pages.

Early in the reign of Cyrus the Great, and during his conquest of the northern provinces of Asia Minor, his general Harpagus was employed in subduing Ionia and the southern provinces. Having conquered the maritime cities of Ionia, Harpagus landed at Halicarnassus, and proceeded to attack the Pedassians*, who in their fortified city, situated at the foot of Mount Lida, were the only Carians that opposed him : they at length submitted, and Harpagus, having incorporated the Ionians, Æolians and Carians with his forces, proceeded against the Lycians. I shall here quote the words of Herodotus† :—

" When Harpagus led his army towards Xanthus, the Lycians boldly advanced to meet him, and, though inferior in number, behaved with the greatest bravery.

---

* On my first arrival at the large town of Moolah, noticed in my Journal of 1838, I approached it from the south-east, having laid down my track over a great extent of unmapped country. My position thus obtained for the town being more than thirty miles from the coast, was declared by those most learned in ancient geography to be too far inland for the city of Pedassus, as that was known to be but six miles from the coast. The recent coast surveys, having carried the Gulf of Cnidus twenty-five miles further inland to the eastward, confirm the position I laid down for Moolah, and my idea of its being the ancient Pedassus, situated on the western termination of the range of Mount Cadmus, the last mountain of which range must have been Mount Lida.

† Beloe's Translation, lib. i. cap. 17 .

Being defeated, and pursued into their city, they collected their wives, children, and valuable effects, into the citadel, and there consumed the whole in one immense fire. They afterwards, uniting themselves under the most solemn curses, made a private sally upon the enemy, and were every man put to death. Of those who now inhabit Lycia, calling themselves Xanthians, the whole are foreigners, eighty families excepted ; these survived the calamity of their country, being at that time absent on some foreign expedition. Thus Xanthus fell into the hands of Harpagus, as also did Caunus, whose people imitated, almost in every respect, the example of the Lycians." This was B.C. 547.

I shall now proceed to the immediate subject of these pages. In my travels in the spring of 1838, I discovered the city of Xanthus, the ancient Arina, the capital of Lycia. To the east of this city*, upon a prominent rock about half a mile from the Acropolis, I found the base of an important structure formed of massive blocks of scaglia, the stone of the country, each weighing from six to ten tons ; this base measured thirty-three feet in length by twenty-two in width : the accompanying view may give a better idea of its position,—one end facing the city conquered by Harpagus and his followers, the other facing nearly due east. Amidst the thicket of vegetation surrounding this base, I was led by a Turk to see the end of a slab of white marble, upon which were

* A ground-plan of the city is published in my ' Xanthian Marbles,' 1843.

sculptured some small figures in procession. This was the only trace of any fallen ruin at that time visible, and I have mentioned it in my published Journal*, at the same time suggesting that a temple must formerly have occupied this cliff. My further researches in Lycia in 1839, and again in 1842 and 1843, aided by the powers of the Government, brought to light the whole ruins of the Monument which had surmounted the existing base.

After puzzling for a long time over the fragments, and reasoning upon various monuments in other parts of Asia Minor, I piled together the Ionic building represented in the frontispiece to these pages, which is drawn from the model presented by me to the British Museum. My reasons for this reconstruction I shall give in detail in the latter part of this account, not wishing here to interrupt the narrative. I may observe that all the fragments excavated from around the base are required for this reconstruction, and that two whole stones only are wanting to complete the Monument ; on drawing together these fragments, no other sculpture of similar art or age is found amidst the ruins of this city, all the rest being either the peculiar art of the early inhabitants, or the well-known sculpture of the imperial Roman and the Christian æra.

In order to carry out the ideas which suggest themselves to me in considering this Monument, I shall assume positions perhaps too bold for the archæologist ; they must however be judged with a regard to the

* 'Asia Minor,' p. 273.

unchanging nature of mankind, and the study of the evidence given in the sequel.

The first impression in viewing this Monument in Lycia, is its being composed in a style and adorned by a character of art *foreign* to that country. The marble is also foreign, probably from Paros : it is the *only* building of the kind I have seen in Lycia. From my observations and sketches during previous travels, I at once recognised the peculiar form of its massive pedestal, surmounted by a temple-like structure, as similar to those which I have *only* seen in Caria in the ancient cities of Alinda, Alabanda and Mylassa. The style of architecture is well known as that of Ionia, the same country. The sculpture, though evidently earlier, is of the same school as the remains of the tomb of Mausolus (353 B.C.) from Halicarnassus, now in the British Museum. The building has been erected as a trophy and tomb : it cannot have been a temple, for in that case the bands of sculpture would have been cut into by a flight of steps, and the statues between the columns would prevent access. The cella will also be seen to be a tomb.

There is no site at Xanthus so well suited for a trophy, commanding the conquered city, as this. It has a fine view of the Acropolis of the Xanthians, from which it is separated by a ravine : the cliff upon which the trophy is placed appears isolated, and affords space for this Monument alone. The existing base, as I have stated, is constructed of massive stones, and may be of a very early date : it resembles the works of the earliest

AL...

TOMBS IN THE NORTH OF CARIA

monuments in the country. In the centre of one end of the superstructure, the end facing the ancient city, I conceive the whole history of the Monument to be told. We see on two stones a continued view of an ancient city, apparently depopulated, a sentinel only being seen on each of the gate-towers. In this represented city I at once recognise the walls and battlements of a Lycian fortification, and within the walls is a stele, one of those monuments almost peculiar to the city of Xanthus*, where four are still standing. Upon the stele, seen over the walls, is placed an emblem,—a sphinx seated between two lions. At the foot of one of these steles, still existing within the walls, I found a seat formed by two lions, which from the tenon under it and the mortise upon the capstone of the stele, must evidently have fallen from it. The walls of this city are represented as surmounting a rock. These combined circumstances leave no doubt in my mind that the city represented is the acropolis of Xanthus.

At the gates, and upon the centre stone of the frieze, is an oriental chief, dressed in a Persian costume and seated upon a Persian throne. Over his head is held by an unarmed attendant an umbrella, the emblem of royalty. Behind his throne is a body-guard of soldiers, in Ionian costume. Before the king, who must be Harpagus, are two unarmed, loose-robed, bearded men, apparently pleading before the chief, whose uplifted arm and general attitude indicate the despotic feeling of a

* One other is seen thrown down at Pinara.

conqueror. Behind these suppliants are assembled the leaders of the Lycians in quiescent attitudes ; differing in this respect from the sculptures upon any other stones, excepting those used to represent the scene described at this end of the Monument ; and each of these stones were found at this, the west end of the base. But we must read this sculptured history more systematically.

On all the four sides of the lower and larger frieze we find a contest between parties, some on foot and others on horseback ; in many figures are recognised the loose-robed, bearded Lycians, with their peculiar arms, their bow-cases, and the leaders or heralds with curtained shields. This I conceive to represent the brave resistance in the plains recorded by Herodotus ; it is evident that the Lycians are generally the vanquished. I shall not here dwell upon the style of art in this frieze, but follow the history.

Upon the smaller and higher sculptured frieze on the south side—for in this frieze each side forms a distinct picture—we find groups of bearded soldiers hastening forwards ; there is a tree, probably to signify the flight as through a forest ; then a jaded horse, clothed with an oriental saddle, and led by a chief in oriental Phrygian cap. The armed soldiers are seen passing behind a bastion, with hands uplifted, and in a supplicating attitude asking refuge within the city, whose portal is guarded by a sentinel. A man is leaning over the tower, evidently inquiring their business. The next stone contains a crowded city, with manned walls ; within these are embattled towers, where females are seen with extended arms : the continuing stone shows the men at the walls, each hurling a stone at assailants at an opposite gate, whence two men, one with the curtained shield of a leader, are making a sally upon assailants in the Ionic Greek costume.

A second picture at the east end represents the mode of attack on another gate of the city. A group of loose-robed, bearded, unarmed and bare-headed peasants tied together are led away captive. These, I think it probable, were spies, or perhaps peasants who had been made to point out a weakly defended part of the city, for which we have precedents at the taking of Sardis and other sieges. They are at all events being led away prisoners from the city, while the Ionians are hastening stealthily, and led on by signs from their leaders, toward the walls of the town. On approaching they crouch down and take off their shoes ; a ladder is placed against the gate-tower, and held with ropes by two men stationed beneath. The Ionian soldiers are seen ascending cautiously and with bare feet, and one of them has arrived at the top of the gates. The architecture of the city again shows a Lycian fortification, and from the panelled windows are seen several heads of the surprised and unarmed people. The north side represents a varied and confused scene, probably the end of a battle after the sally from the city : one group, including a wounded hero led away by a youth, is extremely interesting and beautiful; several figures are seen pointing, as if giving commands, and the combatants are turned and engaged in different directions,—not advancing in order, as seen upon the other sides. One figure is carrying a stool or throne, and another an umbrella inclined over his shoulder. This may represent the removal of the emblems of Persian royalty into the conquered city. The fourth and last side facing the west shows the conquered city, at the gate of which Harpagus is seated upon a throne, and canopied by the royal umbrella, as before described.

For many suggestions in explanation of the next portion of the structure, I am indebted to a learned and ingenious paper read before the Royal Society of Antiquaries in London, in February 1848, by my friend Mr. Benjamin Gibson of Rome. He tells us that ten cities of Ionia supplied Harpagus with troops. Here we have between the columns ten statues, apparently of the same female figure,—perhaps Venus, the popular deity of Ionia; each of these statues is borne up by an emblem beneath its feet; and these emblems Mr. Gibson detects as being the same as those seen on the coins of the maritime cities of Ionia,—the crab of Cos, the dove of Cnidus, the snake of Miletus, the dolphin of Myrina, the phoca of Phocæa, and the shell of Pyrnus. The other statues are too much mutilated for us to determine their emblems. The four lions at the angles are supposed to represent the whole country of the Milesians. We thus have registered, as it were, the arms of the different cities engaged in this conquest, surmounted by the tutelary deity of the country.

On the sculptured architrave of one end is seen a procession carrying offerings usually made by the Greeks, while at the other end is a procession of figures in the loose trowsers worn by the Persians, and carrying the offerings peculiar to that nation. On one side is a hunting-scene, upon the other a battle of equestrians. We have only half the tympanum of the west end, containing beautifully sculptured figures on foot, who have contended with others on horseback : the fore-leg of the horse is seen crossing the shield of the foremost figure. On the tympanum at the east end we have a male and female deity seated opposite to each other, with their attendants, and in the angle a crouching dog. Surmounting the apex of this pediment is a group of three boys, which Mr. Gibson suggests may represent Cares, Lydus and Mysus, the legendary founders of the provinces of Caria, Lydia and Mysia,—thus giving nationality to the whole Monument. The frieze of the cella represents the usual sacrifices and funereal feasts of the Greeks, but none of those ceremonies sculptured on so many of the Lycian tombs.

Had Herodotus of Halicarnassus sought the most natural and legitimate source for this part of his history, he could not have done better than visit and describe the scene represented upon this Monument ; and I do not think it improbable that we have in Herodotus a recital of the events recorded in these friezes, rather than

in the latter an illustration of the historian : we must
bear in mind that the conquest was made about a hun-
dred years before the time of Herodotus.

When I consider the situation, the foreign character,
the evident object, and the graphic detail of all the parts
of this Monument,—the represented architecture, costume, mode of attack, almost the portraiture of the people, all apparently fresh in the mind of the sculptor, and
more particularly the unchanging character of human
nature, ever prone to flatter the feelings and vanity of
the living,—I cannot but attribute the erection of this
structure to the followers of Harpagus, commemora-
ting his victory and serving as a tomb for his heroes : its
erection during the lifetime of some of the conquerors
would probably not be later than 500 b.c. I shall con-
tinue the history of this Monument from observation
and reasoning, and again refer the reader to the sequel
for my authority.

After its conquest, Xanthus was occupied, I believe,
by a people who continued the use of the same architecture and language as their predecessors ; and there
is no trace, except in this Monument, of the continued
residence of an Ionic Greek population,—scarcely a
Greek inscription referable to an earlier date than the
age of Alexander (355 b.c.). I find however almost
continuous monuments, inscriptions and coins in the
Lycian art down to that age,—from the tomb of the son
of Harpagus, to the decree of Pixodarus, king of Caria,
340 b.c.

I find no work of art remaining at Xanthus, referable to the next two centuries: the well-known Greek
coins of the Lycian league, found so abundantly in the
other cities of Lycia, are not met with here; but we
have the coins of Claudius, Trajan, the Antonines, Com-
modus, Severus, Gordian, Aurelian, Constantine and
Julian. I therefore believe Xanthus to have been but a
small city, scarcely issuing coins for a period of several
centuries, while the other cities of Lycia seem to have
risen into greater importance. A little before the Christian æra, Xanthus seems to have revived under the
auspices of Roman protection, and to about the time of
Vespasian (A.D. 80) I attribute many of its most important buildings, the materials of the ruins of which are
still found in abundance. During the next three centuries Xanthus became a great Christian city. Many
buildings of the time of Vespasian seem to have been
pulled to pieces and reconstructed for other purposes:
the seats of the theatre are piled up into walls and bas-
tions, and for the first time united with cement. An
extended city is walled in with blocks and pedestals,
the work of the Greeks, inscribed in honour of their
victors in the Roman games. Numerous churches and
religious establishments are built of the same materials.
I have seen no stones re-worked by this later people;
but columns and doorways, varying in dimensions, are
used in the construction of the same Christian church.
The tombs of this age seem to have been more respected,
and still remain in several directions near the city. This

age of architectural transformation continued until the fifth century of our æra, when we find Xanthus still celebrated for its schools*.

At this period our Trophy Monument stood in ruins upon its cliff, with the statues mutilated by the surrounding iconoclast inhabitants; the heads were broken from the statues, the roof had fallen in, the cella mostly removed, but the pediments and columns were standing. Mr. W. W. Lloyd† ingeniously suggests that it was probably seen in this state by Proclus, A.D. 412, and supposes that Proclus describes the sculptures of the eastern pediment. At this time there were a number of small houses, occupied by Christians, at the foot of the cliff upon which the Trophy Monument stood ; into some of the walls around these houses the stones of the cella were built, but the temple-like Monument still towered above them. At this period an unforeseen and awful visitation awaited this and many neighbouring cities of Asia Minor : earthquakes, shaking even the massive monuments of the early Lycians, threw down and destroyed every building of the Greeks and Christians, and the whole city of Xanthus lay in ruins; not a marble fragment of the superstructure described in these pages remained upon its base, and the ruins buried the houses below; these ruins have perhaps never been visited, certainly they were never moved, until I discovered them in 1838.

* Proclus.   † 'Xanthian Marbles,' W. W. Lloyd, 1845, p. 12.

I feel that this is a daring and perhaps incautious sketch, involving many highly important points in history and in the history of Art; but I am anxious to register my evidence, derived from observation on the spot, and to court discussion upon the various subjects involved in the inquiry. If my position be admitted, the evident similarity of the sculpture of many groups in the larger frieze, as well as in the treatment of the statues, to the Athenian and Phygalian sculptures, must convict these later workmen of plagiarism, and, as hinted by Pausanias, lead us to suppose that Pericles, wishing to adorn Athens, sent to Asia Minor for workmen. This Monument would indicate the employment of Ionians as the designers of the finest of Athenian works.

FURTHER DETAILS RESPECTING

THE TROPHY MONUMENT.

THE following pages are extracted from a paper presented, with the model of the Monument, to the Trustees
of the British Museum in May 1845*.

"The stoa, or base of the Monument shown in the
view upon the pedestal of the model, the site of which
has been already described in my paper, given in to the
Museum, of the Xanthian Expedition, consisted of masses
of scaglia, the stone of the country, weighing from six to
ten tons each ; these so far remain *in situ*, that we ascer-
tain the precise size of the base to have been thirty-
three feet long by twenty-two feet wide : the stones of
the upper course now remaining are set-in three inches,
reducing the area to 32·6 by 21·6 ; this supplies us with
the form of the Monument and the maximum limit of
its scale. I must mention that no other base is to be
found near, and that the sculptures from their position
must all have fallen from this by one sudden convul-
sion ; the small fragments lying with the slabs from
which they have been chipped, and the bronze ties,
run-in with lead, still found in the blocks of marble.

"I must now refer to the ground-plan upon the other

* In giving these pages to the press, some slight verbal alterations
have been made, in order to render the statement more clear.

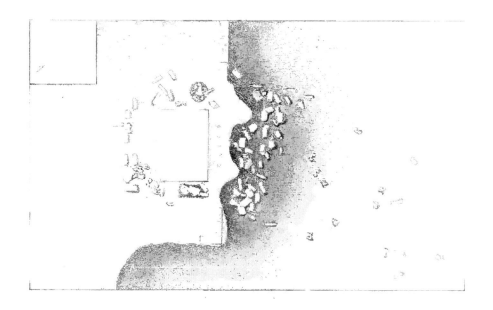

side of the pedestal, showing the fallen sculptures and their position as exposed by excavation: the reasonings from this are also borne out by the position of the unsculptured fragments which are not noticed in this plan.

" In viewing this plan, the first striking feature is the presence of four distinct friezes or bands of sculpture, each having right-angle stones with the bas-reliefs upon the exterior. To place these all upon one small building appeared at first impossible, but their position showed that they had fallen pell-mell, and I had simply the fact to deal with, without regard to precedent: the width of these friezes respectively was three feet three inches, two feet, one foot seven inches, and one foot five inches; the two former being decidedly too wide and heavy to have been supported by the fluted columns, only one foot two inches in diameter, found amongst them.

" My first experiment was cutting, to a scale, pieces of wood resembling each part of the friezes. I commenced by what I have called, from the subject of the bas-reliefs, the City Frieze, two feet wide: of this I had the four corner stones, and on placing them I observed that the subject of the sculptures varied on each side, suddenly changing at the angles and forming four distinct views, each side complete in itself: the stones are of two lengths, four feet eight inches and four feet three inches, or varying slightly from this. After shifting these stones repeatedly, I succeeded in arranging them in a parallelogram, nineteen feet nine

inches wide and twenty-eight feet long, when the view
on each side became complete in itself, one end representing quiescent objects, none of the stones of which
could be used in the tumults seen on the other sides:
this gave me confidence in my arrangement, which was
entirely confirmed by considering that, if I were called
upon to use one more of even the smallest stones, the
frieze must have been too large for the base upon which
it certainly stood: I thus learned that I possessed the
whole, and at once obtained a girth or band giving me
the exact size of the building. I proceeded with the
larger frieze, and by careful combination, aided by three
of the corner stones, I arranged a parallelogram pre-
cisely the size of the former: in this frieze one of the
angles and one of the side stones are wanting; I have
therefore supplied their places by stones of a similar
size to those we possess, thus taking a liberty which
makes this band less valuable as an evidence of the size
of my building than the former; but abundant proof of
this will be repeated when I come to the superstructure.
From the nature of the subject in the bas-reliefs upon
this frieze, one stone is not so evidently united with the
other as in the former frieze.

"I next observed a cornice composed of blocks of
egg-moulding, on the upper surface of which were the
marks of columns and holes for the plinths of statues
or objects placed alternately with the columns; the
depth and singular forms of these cuttings corresponded
with the plinths under the statues lying around. Al-

though prepossessed with the opinion that this description of cornice should be supported by columns, instead of itself forming a base for them to stand upon, I yielded to facts, and had long to consider how to pile these into a single building.

"Thinking over my various sketches made in other parts of Asia Minor, I observed those of the monuments of a city in the north of Caria, which I discovered to be the ancient Alinda; here I found large pedestals and evident marks of their having had superstructures. At Mylassa, twenty-five miles distant, a pedestal of similar construction has its superstructure remaining; and again, at Alinda, is one on a scale nearly as large as the Monument now under consideration. These are all finished with handsome broad cornices, not a fragment of which architectural member is found in the ruins at Xanthus. It occurred to me that the two large friezes might supply this deficiency, and by placing them upon the given base, always keeping in mind the larger pedestal at Alinda as my guide for proportions, I produced, by adding the egg-moulding (a depth of one foot two inches) to the two-foot frieze, a harmony of proportion in the width of the two cornices which I do not think unpleasing. With regard to the blank stones placed between the friezes I am not quite confident, and am in some degree guided by the common remarks of the sailors, who, after having worked for some time to get out a block of marble, which resembled in every respect the large sculptured frieze, reported, ' that it was again

c 2

a blank, and they thought we had two blanks to one prize.' I myself think that the plain blocks exceeded in number the sculptured ones; and from their being the most serviceable to the wants of the succeeding inhabitants, they are the more likely to have been diminished in number; the number cannot have been increased. By the introduction of two courses I have the proportions of my type at Alinda, and thus is formed a pedestal with unbroken bands of frieze, which therefore cannot have had any approach by steps; nor do I conceive it possible that the frieze would have been abruptly broken through by a doorway. I mention this, as the vacant space of one stone may be supposed to have been left to form a doorway; but we have, I think, fragments even of this sculptured stone. The following argument however is in my opinion conclusive on this point. In the view of the base, massive stones are seen still remaining above the level of the upper course upon which we place the friezes. Time and Turks, and from my own experience I must add English sailors, roll down such stones, but these agents never raise them up; the pile has no doubt been higher, but surely not lower than at present. Again, each of the stones of the friezes used are left rough within, and not squared at the inner angles; while the other friezes, of which we shall speak hereafter, are finished inside with a smooth surface and moulding; I therefore conclude that this pedestal was solid, and thus adapted to support the structure we are about to place upon it.

" I have stated that upon the upper side of the stones
of the cornice of egg-moulding are seen the marks of
alternate statues and columns. From a corner-stone
of this we obtain the exact position of the base of the
column upon it, and are enabled to measure the space
between the columns, thus ascertaining the intercolumniation. Having the bases and capitals of the columns,
it is easy to raise the building as high as the architrave. At this stage I observed that the next frieze or
sculptured architrave, having both the inner and outer
sides finished with a cornice, was composed of four
distinct subjects: one a battle, of which we have four
stones; another a hunting-scene, also of four stones;
a third, representing a Persian offering, consisting of
three stones only, the figures being half upon one
stone and half upon the adjoining one, and each of
these showing a groove or cutting on the lower edge,
ceasing abruptly nine inches from the ends, and thus
forming a square solid bed of eighteen inches to rest
upon the capital of the column beneath; there were
three more stones of a similar form, the bas-reliefs
representing a Greek offering. These again give the
intercolumniation, which agrees with that of the bases.
The length of the stones requiring support at their junction also fixes the number of columns upon the ends
and sides.

" In the excavations we found seven regular Ionic
capitals, and only a fragment of one with a horn or
volute projecting from the angle; this one necessarily

implies the existence of four, making eleven out of
fourteen required for the model: eleven would be too
many for the porticos only, and I have therefore placed
columns at the sides, concluding that the three capitals
are missing. The next stage of our building is not a
matter of doubt, but of unaccountable singularity: we
have only two small fragments of one or two of the
dentils which must have surrounded this part of the
Monument; the marks made by the dentils on the
under side of the cornice which rested on them is the
evidence upon which I rest my introduction of them:
above this portion of the cornice is its crowning member, having lions' heads to spout the water from the
gutter within. The angle-stone of this is important,
as it shows upon its back the inclination and width
of three successive tiles, which were of white marble,
and in this case of the same piece as the inclining cornice of the pediment: near the lower part is also seen
the cutting to receive the pedestal of a statue which
stood at the angle, the acroteria. Another stone of
this cornice is equally important as showing the angle
of the pediment; it formed the keystone or saddle,
and had upon it the hollow to receive the pedestal
of a statue on the apex of the pediment. The ridge-
tiles of marble apparently covering the junction of the
flat tiles, and the crowning ornament upon the ridge of
the roof, with the dipping ridge-tiles projecting from
its opposite sides, complete the covering of the Monument. We found beneath each end the sculptured

tympana, the angles of which, carried out, exactly fill the pediments, and confirm the dimensions afforded by the various friezes and the standing base.

"We have still our frieze left, with four sculptured angles, the subject of the bas-reliefs representing the funereal ceremonies. One stone of this, eight feet nine inches long, forming with the sculptured angle of the side-stone a length of nine feet six inches, I place as the frieze of one end of the cella of the Monument, resting the two ends upon the capitals of pilasters, which from their form must have been those of the antæ of a cella: of these I found three. Of the side-stones of the frieze I contrive suitable subjects, guided by the sculptures, and form lengths of fifteen feet, making a parallelogram fifteen feet by nine feet six inches. Placing this in the centre of the building, I find that the stones of my ceiling, each with two panels or coffers, exactly reach from the architrave to the cella, resting upon each of the friezes; this again confirms my arrangement. The entrances to the cella—in this case probably a sepulchre—are shown by the discovery of a stone of this form :

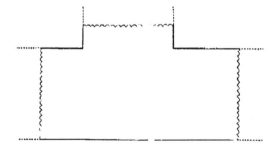

We also find an ornament or mantling which was over a doorway. I must remark that we saw only a very small portion of the plain stones required to form the walls of the cella; but being plain and not very large, they would have been, as before observed, more desirable for the use of succeeding inhabitants. We have fragments of the bases of the pilasters.

" The building being now erected, I proceeded to the arrangement of the statues, for which I had no theory, but began by placing each above the position in which I found it in the earth. The statues are of two sizes: the smaller, of which we have six, from their attitudes as well as their lying at both ends of the building, had evidently fallen from the top of the pediment; and on examination I observed that they were weatherbeaten all round, showing that they had filled an exposed position. I can have no doubt of the correctness of this arrangement. The next figures are lions, one of which had fallen from either angle of the west end: I replaced them in that position between the columns, and found that their projecting noses alone have been subjected to the corroding action of the weather, and that their bodies within the colonades are uninjured. At the east end I found the paws of one lion and the flanks of another, which doubtless filled the spaces corresponding with the western end. I then raised the several statues to the vacant spaces between the columns nearest to them, and again found that those parts alone of the bodies and drapery which would have projected from between the columns show the effect of the rain and wind, the rest of the figures retaining the smooth surface of the marble. Each of these statues is borne by an emblematic animal, and the drapery is blown violently by the wind. The Monument now put together requires but two whole stones to complete the larger frieze, and one to complete the west tympanum. We should then have the whole of the four friezes, the pediments and necessary architectural members, and every niche and pedestal for the reception of statues occupied by the fragmental representation of such statue."

My reasons for placing the pavement around the Monument at the level represented, concealing a considerable portion of the massive base now exposed, are the following :—

At the assumed level, in excavating on the north side, we ceased to find the fallen fragments of the building, and soon afterwards lost all trace of the chips of broken marble ; we then came to a dark-coloured native earth, on the surface of which we found several bronze and bone pins, arrow-heads, &c. The cisterns found at the east and west ends of the base of the building have been arched over ; the crowns of these arches forming the same level, which corresponded with that of the dark earth on the north side. The level adopted has also the advantage of placing the eye of the spectator on

D

a line with the lower part of the sculptured frieze; whereas, had a lower one been chosen, the set-off in the massive base would have intercepted a perfect view of the sculpture.

During the whole of the excavations, although we found the limbs, feet, fingers and drapery of the statues, we never discovered a fragment of the heads,—not a curl or feature, not an ear, a nose, or any chip of the heads of the statues, notwithstanding a careful examination of the earth surrounding the ruins. The reason for this did not occur to me at the time, and I urged the men to persevere until they should lay bare the rock; thinking it possible that the heads might have first fallen, and their broken fragments have been shaken down among the blocks, and that they might still lie concealed below. Instead of finding the expected pudding-stone rock, we came upon small irregular stones, artificially cemented together; and on advancing, we found regular walls forming a series of small houses; in these, near the openings left for doorways, were decayed iron hinges, bolts, rings, and numerous nails; in the houses, weights, scales, and broken pottery. Upon the tiles of the floors were imprinted patterns, and amongst them the Cross of the early Christians was conspicuous; whilst upon some of the walls the Panagia of the Greek church was still to be recognised. This circumstance is interesting, as affording relative dates for the existence of the various buildings, and a probable explanation of the absence of the heads of the statues, as we know that during the third and fourth centuries the Greek Christians generally were iconoclasts. In the spring of 1846 upwards of thirty heads of statues were discovered in a well near Smyrna, doubtless thrown there from the same religious motives which caused the mutilation of the statues in this Monument. The hatred seems to have been limited to the heads of statues; the limbs are not injured, nor were the heads of the figures in bas-relief ever destroyed. There is one head of a boy in the group on the apex of the east pediment which has escaped, possibly from its high position upon the Monument. The incidents which occurred whilst I was engaged in watching with care the progress of these excavations, have afforded me the means of reasoning and drawing the conclusions offered in the early part of these pages.

THE END.

PRINTED BY

RICHARD AND JOHN EDWARD TAYLOR,

RED LION COURT, FLEET STREET.

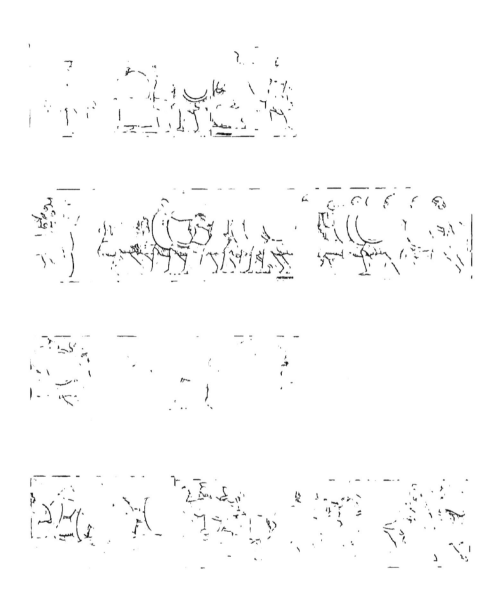

[redacted]

Lightning Source UK Ltd.
Milton Keynes UK
UKHW02f0534310518
323512UK00004B/287/P

9 781378 605301